# SORES AND ROSES

by

FRITZ HAMILTON

Downtown Poets' Coop New York

Cover drawing and design: James Nolan

Photograph: Paul Henning

Issued in limited edition.



Published by X-press Press for the Downtown Poets' Coop, Brooklyn, N.Y.

*ISBN* 0-917402-08-1

Member: COSMEP

**Produced at The Print Center, Inc., Box 1050, Brooklyn, N.Y. 11202, a non-profit printing facility for literary and arts-related publications. Funded by The New York State Council on the Arts and the National Endowment for the Arts.**

For Rissa Korsun
who
gave me my 1st poetry reading
who
published my 1st book
who
took me shrieking to my 1st
madhouse /
you
who were my NY mama . . .
in
memoriam
. . .
!

Previously published

*The Street and the Joint*

*The Plunge*

*Redman is Redman's Mommy*

The poet, Mr. Hamilton, gives special thanks to David Gershator, who helped edit and arrange *Sores and Roses* (and thought up its title), and to Michael Welch, for her poem from which he quotes in "To Your Aging Poem on My Wall"; and to James Nolan for his art work and Paul Henning for his photograph, and to *Scree* magazine that first published "Dawn over Dead Neon!" and "Trying To Do Good," and to WBAI radio that first broadcast "Detroit Pat!" and "Coming Home to a Party!"

## Bowery Champ

Well
sure is something standing
at Peter Cooper's statue off
the Bowery trying
to read his roman
numeral dates when

this
dignified derelict/ small
kind of neat in his
torn tacky sweater carrying
his worth in a
shopping bag steps
to me grumbles

"Man, I gave you my
autograph back in
Chicago, I'm
Johnny Bratton, made

a million in
the ring, my
mother died, man, they

thought I was
crazy but
it was the clot, a
blood clot, baby, that's
all, you

give me a
dollar
man
?"

and
he's off

straight and solid like
Peter Cooper's stone
me

still remembering
Smedley's bar in
Chicago/ me
drunk among fighters

Johnny Bratton and
Ezzard Charles passing
through (Charles
with his slow fatal illness
moving on a cane) I

scale the fence to
Peter Cooper's monument and
with my pen scrawl
"Johnny Bratton" on
its base/ wonder

why
I couldn't give him the
dollar . . .
?

## Rodney

Well
man/ me
in and out of psych wards and
drunk tanks for
the past three yrs/ can't
hold a job more'n
two, three days maybe before
I got to tie one on and
sometimes
don't even get back to
get my pay
so
fresh out of Bernstein detox waitin'
for my Welfare check to
come/ don't
got no money till it do and
too sick to work/ my
caseworker
she get me this room on
14th St./ just
a chair, a dresser, and
a bed/ with
a window facin' the back of
this bldg on 13th St.
and
I sit all day starin' at
my dirty wall till
out
from under the bed crawl
this big black rat and
he sit real quiet there beside
the radiator lookin'
up at me with
me starin' back down at him and
pretty soon we got this
understandin'/ I
won't do nothin' to him if

he don't do nothin' to me
then
he go back disappear under
the bed and
for days after I sit starin'
down at the floor lookin'
for him but
he don't come out and
I'm thinkin'/ me
almost 45-yrs-old and
gettin' a little tired of
these one night stands/
                    maybe
if I just spruce the place up
a little and
put a plate of good food beside
the radiator
            . . .
              but
shit!
he ain't comin' back/ I
just go out and get me a
little Gypsy Rose wine to
forget . . .
!

## The Favorite

"Well, Prof. Jonesboro, would
you please tell me
now
that your head is crushed like
a boomerang/ face
covered with gray stubble over
the wine sores and
your
fly is open/pants
too small up to your knees sopped
with piss/ legs
wasted down to poles like
your arms/ no
socks for
your torn left sneaker and
your worn right army boot
hair
once curly red (pride
of all the ladies in
the Humanities Dept.) now
a mat of white
filth falling
like greasy snakes beside
the majestic boomerang/ 2
red madhouses screaming
from your crumbled skull/ nose
so recently aquiline with
dignity now
ground horsemeat hooked
sideways/ you
Prof. Jonesboro released
by the university for
not attending your classes and
thrown
from your home by
your beloved wife who

could not stand you beating
the children you love/ you
Prof. Jonesboro/ favored
by everybody in
faculty and student body
what
are you doing with that
pint of Wild Irish Rose sitting
in your urine in
the middle of Broadway for
the scrutiny of your
horrified ex-students and
ex-colleagues. . .
?"

"Writing
a
book
!"

## NY Summer Day

Walking
slowly along 14th St.
gasping unable
to distill the NY summer air
army
of ravaged soldiers pounding
through
the torn battlefield of my skull
sewer
of beer and bad whiskey beating
my rusted entrails like
refuse from the garbage dump off
the side of Gansevoort Pier
leaning
against the window of a bar
bent back pouring
a Colt 45 down my rotting hole
trying
to wash the poison out
to
petrify the pickled corpse
greasy sweat popping
from my face in globules losing
their cohesion to
itch a river down my skin
sidewalk an
errant washboard on a sea of phlegm
tilts
back and forth I
wrap about a Lindsay trash basket to
keep from falling in
the poison of my vomit
a dead rat among putrid vegetable below
my face
I marinate the stew with
last night's bilious gesture

and
walk on but
can't
walk on
can't move
me
up against
pinioned against
a cement sea
trying
to think what to do
street sounds now
where am I
yes . . .
a shoe slides past my eyes
yes yes . . .
on the sidewalk yes . . .
my face
yes . . .
yes . . .
down on something wet
yes . . .
!
I sit up quickly and
wipe it from me
dogshit!
my NY pillow
I look around me
sonofabitch
I lost my Colt 45 . . .
!

## New York Morning

In
the dry Spring fountain of
Washington Sq Pk
black

derelict with trumpet as-
phyxiating the mouthpiece blowing
out a lonely taps/ black
raincoat flapping tired pigeons over

piss-drooping pants/ no
one caring as
the morning April shadow
boxes through the wiry

trees dancing on
cement/ rubble
of New York City playing
at his feet/ an

aging
urchin sleeping
off the wine on
cement beside him

black
bottle gang already forming on
the other side of the fountain
2 cops

strolling their
dull curiosity through
the rabble/ all
celebrated by

the trumpet wandering

into unsuspected notes/ other
forms of sleep/ a
toddler in

a red jacket pulls her
wooden doggy by
think-
ing of mama and

chocolate Easter . . .
!

## Good Feeling

Soup
all watered this
morning (or
so it seems) at
Everything for Everybody after

standing in line in
a sub-zero NY chill
wind
freezing your soul like
a Bowery stiff in December and

the workers from the adjoining
meat packer taunt you from
their bloody aprons and
the soup is cold piss with
a few beans and carrots floating

in it like
something scoured up from
the burnt bottom of the pot and
old Jesus next to you smells like
his vomit down

his torn black coat and
he keeps trying to
elbow you off the
bench while
the angry waif snarls over

the pot and
drips your soup over her
dirty fingers before
setting it in its
dirty bowl with

a dirty spoon on

the dirty counter before you but
that doesn't make you mad until
the sad waif puts
your bread right in

a pool of last night's
rotting swill (or
God knows what) beside
your bowl
so

you take the filthy slop and
hold it to your wasted
dick and warm it with your
piss as everybody around
you howls like

a sty full of wild pigs and
now you're back out freezing in
front of the packinghouse and
you're 86ed from
Everything for Everybody and

your stomach feels repentant but
at least your heart feels
pretty good . . .
!

## Girl at Morning Soup Line

Small
pleasant hand putting
the soup and
peanut butter cookie before
me/ telling

me about the coffee I
can get in back
smiling
letting me know I'm
worth something at

breakfast with the
beaten and forgotten at
Everything for Everybody and
suddenly
the counter filled with

wayward crumbs and
defeated dirty fingers is
a small garden in
Barrington, Ill., and
I

look up over my
bowl to see
young Janet (a
high school crush who
never touched me/ round

Dutch face/ freckled/ healthy
flower garden of
its own) and
the soup filled with

spinach and

potatoes and
green beans still crisp starts
to taste awfully good and
I
want to ask her

"Are you Janet?" knowing

that she is (even
if she says she
isn't . . . . ) and
the line of derelicts along
the counter becomes

the row of dancing birch trees that
lined Taylor Rd and
the stench of
wine-sopped bodies is
the dusty weed and lilac blown

hot from the field in
my sunburnt face

"Are you really Janet?" knowing

that she has to be (already
more love than
Janet ever gave me) and
I
rise to leave hanging

my number on a
nail (marveling at
its bloodlessness) and

she smiles again and
says

"Goodbye now, come back." and

I step outside to
try on the free shoes on
the rack as

the worker from a nearby
packing plant laughs at me but
I feel too good to
care . . .
!

## Frozen Alley

Holy
Jesus never in
my 7 yrs just
passin' through this
fuckin' Bowery have

I
seen nothin' like
fat Fleishman sittin'
naked on this garbage can all

smilin' through his
big rubber head in
this alley with

zero degrees pumpin'
60 through
the garbage/ fat

Fleishman havin'
taken off all his clothes just
ridin' this garbage can/ his
ass sure frozen to the top

holdin'
his pint of Wild Irish peach freezin'
to death and
not carin' and

just last wk little ol'
Nick found passed
out sleepin' back here stiff like
a frozen fish/ so

I say/ near
frozen to death myself

"Fleishman
follow my ass on
to the mission . . . "

but
then I seen it/ Fleishman
holdin' this bloody shattered
bottle and

blood frozen all
over his legs and
groin. . . .

*Shit!*
Fleishman done cut
off his own

balls
!

## Paul

Okay
all wk long stay with my
hysterical woman while
she
scratches out her MA thesis screaming
at me and
not givin' me no lovin' so
I gulp my half-gallons of Gallo wine and
write her these
tender love songs then
her thesis done/ she
calls me an asshole and
throws me out of the house with
instructions never to see her again
so
I get blotto at Jimmy's bar then
take the CTA north to
pick up this sweet skank at the
Wise Fools Pub then
change the names on my tender love
songs in
order to melt her skanky bent which
done/ me
and the skank and a fifth of
Fleischmann's gin/ we
all pile in her old Ford pickup and
head stinko up to her cabin in
Madison where
I blackout and awake with my wrists
somehow slit and
my skank (not
givin' me no lovin' I'm sure) sleeping
troubled in the next room only
to wake up bitter and hungover to
call me an asshole and throw me out of
the house with

instructions never to see her again so
I just drink up the rest of my money in
a Madison bar knowing
none of this would have happened if
I'd of got some lovin'
so
me and a pint of Fleischmann's we
hitch on back to Chicago where
I hysterically go right back to my
hysterical woman/ tears
of remorse gushing down my wretched
cheeks and
wail

"Baby, love me! Love me!"

and
slyly shove my love
songs into her calloused paw but
*shit!*
I forgot to change back the
names . . . and
I suspect once again I
ain't gonna get no
lovin'!

## Dawn over Dead Neon!

"Welcome
to 42nd St. the
world's greatest
MOVIE CENTER" above

the Victory theatre marquee at
6:00 a.m./ gay
junkies shirtless in
red bandannas/ teenage

Puerto Rican hustlers strolling
by with beer/ old
toothless hooker striding
scoreless from the

neon-peppered Orange Julius
children
feigning a fight beneath
"The Private Afternoons of

Pamela Mann"/ skinny
red-shirted pimp glistening
black-skinned against
the ticket window of

4X hit "Intimate
Teenagers"/ winehead
cross-legged sitting in
a beer case thinking of

the class in Victorian lit he'll
never teach again
black
boys hopped-up near-

crazy clustered about
a pair of dice beneath

Charles Bronson in
"The Stone Killer"/ 2

pallid tramps in
gowns cut to their bellies am-
bling arm-in-arm (with
somebody's frail black boy hooked

straggling between them) 3
sick Jesus children brandishing
big crosses beneath
Wang Ping in

"Five Fingers of
Death"/ tired
hungover old man in
dirty white shirt hang-

ing his breakfast
special "2 fresh country
eggs 60¢ . . . ." in
front of the

Western Beefburger cafe as
the hungry woman with
long gray coat and
one sneaker only looks

on/as
the angry black drifter with
half a nose and
high black boots shining

their spit looks
on/ as
Gene Hackman in
"Night Moves" looks

on/greasy

70 degree morning blowing
the flies along 42nd St./ dust
darkening the vomit and

wino piss and
crushed cigarette box as

"Women in Cell Block 7" and

"The Hitchhiker" and

"The Last Days of Man on
Earth" look

on . . .
!

## Trying To Do Good

Old
Cyrus the pimp (beyond
the ardors of his
trade) carries

his newspaper bag full
of *Watchtowers* along
42nd St. trying
to sell them to

the whores and hustlers/ all
the honky tonk urchins of
his street (tired
bone relique of

his sordid days before
the bust and
10 yrs in Attica for
hustling dope and

jail bait pussy) Cyrus
back with the word trying
to do good/ steps
hot

mid-afternoon into
a bar his girls once
worked/ to
take a crap/ his

old barkeep friend Murphy
seeing him/ throwing
him out with
his bag of Godliness

Cyrus
standing outside the

door listening
to the laughter

squatting
dog-like in the doorway to
leave his pile of thanks
wiping

his ass with
a front page tissue from
the latest
                issue . . . .

## Growlin' Garrett

Well
man, just
me and my pint of Richard's sittin'
on this stoop across from
my crib/

just
watchin' the hot flow of
manhood goin' in and out for
my good Wanda/

who
done throwed me out with
my wine to
make her bread through
their flow/

me
a drinkin' just
thinkin' about it watchin'
it all happen/

sometimes
more'n 10 dudes flowin'
in to see my
Wanda/

until
me gettin' so shook
up about to
shake apart/

so
go across to
my Wanda's door and wait and

this big dude come out lookin'

so peaceful zippin'
up his fly
and

I push myself right
mad up in his face and
growl

"Hey, Jack, gimme
a half-dollar for
some wine . . .
!"

## Jerry

Right
foot froze off sleepin'
in the doorway of the
Monterrey Hotel/ winter

of '67 . . . then
all the toes on my
left foot froze off sleepin'
in Central Pk/ winter

of '72 . . . then
spend Xmas of '74 in
St. Vincent's Hosp as
they saw off my left

leg full of gangrene froze
sleepin' in 7th St. outside of
McSorley's Alehouse
now

me in my wheelchair all
the time in
the Majestic Bar with
nothin'

to do but drink up my
disability check and
flop
at the Palace Hotel like

I paid my dues, man, but
now I got it
made . . .
!

## Lily True Love

I'm
little Lily/ once
the sweetest, most popular blonde in
all Chicago/ all
the men wanting me/ a constant
string of suitors and
I take for a husband the
handsomest and most gifted man on
the Southwest Side/ big
Eddy Longbrow with
his MBA from the U.of I./ three
yrs a halfback on the Illini, even
starring in a Rose Bowl Game and
from the beginning
my fine husband never makes it home before
2:00 a.m. (if
at all) and
he's always drunk (sometimes
smelling of another woman) me
having to somehow roll him into
bed and
then somehow roll him back
out again by 7:00 a.m. to make it to
his executive job/ which
gets harder and harder for me to
do until Eddy gets fired and
even though his next job is even better he
still can't make it to work half
the time so he loses it too/ and
this goes on for over 10 yrs until
he can't even hold down a position as
shoe salesman/ so
I have to work as a secretary while
Eddy stays home with the children and
the baby sitter while
he drinks (always
managing to get off to a bar before

I come home to scold him)

and

eventually this handsome, powerful
man grows fat and shapeless/ too sick even
to make the bars and
after a series of hospitalizations, the
doctor tells him to stop drinking or
die . . . *so he stops!* and
his health and good looks return and
he starts holding this beautiful job and
taking a real interest in me and
the children/ *like*
*where's my big baby to take care of*
*now?/*

so

one fine Saturday night I
just give him a big kiss and whisper
"I'm so proud of you, Eddy, and
love you so much!" and
hand him a nice cold
beer . . .
!

## Loversilly Bill

Hanging
out behind the Majestic Bar by
his neck/ red
eyes and

purple swollen tongue pressing
from their orifices
big
Loversilly Bill/ over

5,000 women in just
10 yrs (or
about 1.4 women per day)
before

the bottle got him and
the money went and
penniless
he found his home at

the Majestic Bar and
a flop at
the Sunshine Hotel
before

swinging
out behind the Majestic Bar
Loversilly Bill with
5,000 notches in his

groin/ pint
of Gypsy Rose sticking up from
his open
fly . . .
!

## Slap Happy Sal

So
every mornin' little
Slap Happy Sal he
enter the Palace Bar/ go
straight to fat Federika bent

drunk and dirty like
stiff crude oil over her wine and
beer and
Slap Happy slap her fat greasy
fanny and shout

"Hey, Federika! How's
the fattest, drunkenest
filthiest street hooker in
Uptown . . .
?"

Federika
not sayin' nothin' just
suckin' up the booze through
her rotten teeth
then

come about noon little
Slap Happy go out to
the alley to sleep
but

once Slap Happy don't make no
alley/ he
just lie down and pass out in
the Palace doorway
well

somebody got to move him so
fat Federika slop on over and

lift her skirt to
crouch over Slap Happy's face and
piss like a bloated ox with
the whole Palace laughin'

but
Slap Happy he
just wake up thinkin'
somebody done spilled some
good wine on him and

he
just lick up all he can before
climbin' right on up to slap
Federika on her fat fanny and
shout

> "Hey, Federika! How's
> the fattest, drunkenest
> filthiest street hooker in
> Uptown . . .
> ?"

so
guess little Slap Happy get
the last laugh after
all . . .
!

## Miller

Every
morning shaking and
sick I
crawl out of my cage at the
Mohawk Hotel all
stinking of puke and cheap
wine and filth/

stomach
trying to bolt up into
my mouth while
the bloody pistons mash
my potato brains and

scratching my sores covered
by clothes unchanged in wks
buy
my pint of Richard's at Rothchild's and
I'm off to my clothing store window
washing job having

to pass the Northwestern Railroad
Station enroute where
I always see my friend Luke standing
in the viaduct beneath the station
waiting
for this old man to come in from
the burbs

(so
Luke, all sick and desperate, can
take this man around a corner for a
little good morning sex for
which
Luke gets enough to buy his
good morning wine)

well

every day, it seems, I'm
more and more getting like Luke until
pretty soon I lose my job and
I can't afford my cage at the Mohawk
Hotel any more

so
hell, I'm as good a man as Luke/ I
go out before the Northwestern
Station and
wait for some man from the burbs for
me to do him like Luke does

and
before long, me sick and about to puke, sure
enough this old man comes up to
me and we go hide around the corner and
I come away with over $50 and
Luke whimpers

"What the hell you do to
get that much?"

and
I just smile and walk away to
the Madison St. bridge to
throw my bloody blade into
the Chicago River/
hell!

what do you expect
?/ I might be a drunk but
I still like
women . . .
?

## Homer Hal

All
day sitting before
the tube in Gus'
Tavern watching

the White Sox/ watching
Zisk and Gamble hit
them out
Hell!

I was out there once/ in
right in Comiskey Pk like
Zisk/ had
eight homers in May/ two

more before the All-
Star Game break
then (average
dropped below 220) back

to Indianapolis never
to return/ released
by the organization two
yrs later . . .

what they never knew was
how I came to the park drunk or
hungover all the time

how
five of those ten homers came
on balls I was
too drunk to see

one
that almost cleared the

upper
        deck

"Wow! Gus, did you see that?
You see that Zisk? I
hit one like that! Remember, Gus?
1952 against the Indians . . .
!"

## Detroit Pat

So
there I am fresh
into New York City about
3 wks from Chicago with
my money gone sitting

in a rm packed with
low dirt drunks wondering
how and if
I'll make it through another second

Winter
licking the Village streets with
a murderous frost-bit
tongue when

in walks this
300-lb Irishman with
round bald head like
a skinned potato filled
with little yellow teeth/ leather

jacket like some
soft diesel semi and
it's Detroit Pat just
in off the line from
the Motor City and

I
ask if he can
put me up for a
night in

lieu of the Bowery and

like a pushcart beside
a moving van I
end
up following Detroit Pat to
his 2 rms on
14th St. and

it's true
the john is downstairs in
the hall so

sometimes Detroit Pat urinates
in his sink (making
the dishes and silverware a
little suspect) but

that's okay cause
it's Detroit Pat's Pad and
next day without
me asking he

goes with me Uptown around
Columbia University where
my clothes, guitar, tons
of manuscript and typewriter are
incarcerated in this
madman's room and

it takes us all day to
muscle it all back down to
14th St. (im-
possible for me to do it by
myself) and



he's really a

monstrous mashed sweet
potato this Pat/ 300 lbs of
care and concern about (of
all things) *me* here
in New York City/ Detroit Pat really

a sensitive Dublin flower garden spread
on everything he
rides quietly over/ this
heavy duty mick/ and

he really isn't much better off than
I/ Chicago Fritz/ but
he lets me have a set of
keys and

I'm home
first time since Chicago and
how do I tell a
300-lb diesel semi from
Detroit I love him without

him thinking me queer/ without
getting myself mashed into
14th St. beneath his
big tire

?/ maybe
I'll just spend my
last dollar at McDonald's for
a Big Mac hamburger and
give him half

I
think he'll
understand . . .

!

## The Best

*for Elbert*

No
question the best among
us at
Income Maintenance no. 13
Juan Oliveros/ tired

of standing for wks in Welfare
lines to have
his records lost and
himself crapped upon by
sadistic bureaucrats inventing
reasons why

Juan Oliveros is
unqualified for
assistance to feed his
8 children and wife who
screams at him day and night

Juan Oliveros/ no
question the best among us picking
up the skinny Jewish bitch's
desk and
throwing it at her fat

black dyke supervisor/ doing
it for the rest of us who
do not draw the bureaucrat's
pay but/ like Juan Oliveros/ get

crapped on by the
sadists who run our noses in it to
give them pleasure as

they run their pens up between
our legs to

write off our balls
Juan
Oliveros/ best
among us as
the desk shatters and

the bitch's papers fall
all over the floor and
the fat black dyke supervisor
wiggles
her clumsy flab shrieking out

the Welfare center door
beautiful
Juan Oliveros now
waiting for the judge to
send him to

Riker's Island for
catching the fat dyke and
ramming
the blade up her fat
ass/ no

question the best/ doing
it for all of us/ his
8 children still hungry/ his
wife in Bellevue madhouse with
her wrists slit . . .
!

**Coming Home to a Party!**
*for Detroit Pat*

Some-
thing rather beautiful walk-
ing late into my
14th St. room to find

gray mice scurrying
under the bed/ behind
my typewriter/ into
my closet/ all

this back-to-nature right
in my own room and
I'm happy that my
banana has a big hole gnawed

into it for
I don't want my loved ones
hungry and
I fall into bed to

listen to my pets dancing
beneath me and
going to the bathroom in
my bag of oranges until

sleepless/ I
turn on my light to find
a rat on my table brushing
his teeth with my toothbrush and

spraying his armpits with
my Rightguard so
I

just give him my

last 10 dollars and
tell him to go out and
have a good time cause
it's so nice to find them

rodents is
just like
people . . .
!

## To Your Aging Poem On My Wall

*for Michael*

*"I am tired.*
*Please come into the room.*
*The dog will greet you*
*And I will play the violin."*

Michael/ you
my great sorry song/ dog
dying in your pretty eyes
know
I cannot be with your
terrible lonely beast and
your violin so
richly sad it tears
too dangerously across my
strings

*"I know that*
*Your hands have played violins today.*
*I hear the violins."*

Yes, Michael, yes, but
my
violin/ my
song of hope/ not
the murderous minor key in
which you work so
sweetly heavy like
the wet black earth upon
our grave

*"I do not know the color of light.*
*I only know the cold when*
*color is absent."*

The frost, Michael, is
on your violin/ you

know this/ how
much
longer must you abuse it/ how
much longer will it
play . . .
?

*"I am tired of turning the pages*
*of the newspaper.*
*The radio is low,*
*And we wait by the door."*

Just
one more page, Michael, to
the obits/ see
the picture of the crying man with
thick red sideburns/ he
who entered your room to
be bit by your dog as
you lay strapped to the bed shrieking
to die/ the tubes of life so
precarious in
your arms and
nose . . .
?

*"Please come into the room.*
*The dog will greet you*
*And I will play the violin."*

The violin lies
busted at
the side of your bed, Michael, the
only Stradivarius I have ever known to
die of a broken heart and
for my own strong heart I
must stay away

*"But I have only the vacant mind,*

*The mathematics of love."*

I know, Michael, I know
I
close the door upon your
bloody dog and
broken violin and
walk into the morning
so
much warmer here on
14th St. as
my early spring starts
to chase away your
winter

*"I am tired.*
*Please come into the room."*

No more, Michael
please
stop your morbid bleeding and
rest quietly/ the sun grows
all too warm now and
the Hudson is just 3
blocks away and I
shall sit upon the pier and
love
the tugs and ocean liners and
the free diving
gulls . . . .

# . . . AND ROSES

## Good Morning after Being with You

Core
of my pear/ your
pear, Jeanne love, lying
on your table fresh
from my lips

as
you too are fresh from
my lips/ you

now wrapped in a
bright towel filled
with funny red tigers
across
the room ironing
your skirt for work

you
the core of my
New York happiness right
now/ everything

pinpointing on your
table with
our breakfast of
fruit and coffee and
hot crossed buns

my
pear void of fruit ly-
ing across a white
napkin like
my baby at
St. James Infirmary

Christ

another day/ time
to let her go, God bless her/ my
coffee cold now/ almost
gone/ your

old gray dog stretched
several feet away for
another night's sleep as
you
retire to your bathroom to
wash your hair/ your

tigers discarded to
fend for themselves on
the floor/ oh well

time
for me to leave/ to
walk into the
waking street

good morning, New York City

time
to survive . . .
!

## Crusade!

Great
scimitar slicing
through my entrails

angry
Saracen stirring
his frothy steed through
me/ my

insides a sick battlefield laid
to waste/ all

the people of 7th Ave. drawing
away like
wary lambs from
a wounded vicious prairie dog leaving

me that much more
isolated in the Village/ beyond
shriek or whimper with
no one prone
to listen

(Jeanne love, if
you must be
angry at me that's
okay/ my

Christian parapets worthy of
withstanding that
onslaught
                but

when you will not tell
me why/ your
Muslim wrath sneaking

up on me in the
dead of night/ my

sleeping army is
left ruined and
dying/ ultimately
a victim of my own
frustration . . . . ) only

the small hungry
prairie dog left to
escape into the
surrounding badlands

perhaps, love
you
will be compassionate and
set a dog biscuit on
your doorstep/ something

to assuage my hunger and
let me know every-
thing is really

all
right . . .
!

## New Old Room

1:37 a.m. in
a new old bed/ room
enough for you (who
are not here) in

my 1st night in this Village room/ my
new NY home/ my
loins still damp from
loving you (NY

howling/ splashing/ grinding through
a soft rain on 14th St.
5 floors to my window creeping in
with the warm
breeze of late February/ celebrating
my 39th birthday/ me
all alone/ still

fresh from being with you/ everything
sweet birth since you/ with
you/ being
                    for me
                                        you . . . .

infants of
every kind and type born
each new moment of
our
wonderful oneness/ how

beautifully fecund and
productive are the
*we*/ I

          reach up and turn
          off the light/ you

my darling, in
every sound and
every smell from

    14th St. as
    I
    shut my

        eyes . . . .

## Wheat Field in Your Womb

Like
the noonday in
a field outside of
Barrington, Ill.

wheat
bending graceful muscle bearing
the powerful life grain

me
a 10-yr-old child buried
deep into the
swishing dance

all
this I feel be-
side you this afternoon naked in

my poor room on 14th St. on
the big lopsided bed with
the spring street noises straight
from Puerto Rico shining

through my dirty window (card-
board covering the
broken pane) whole

vast wheat field swimming in
your womb as I (still
the small child buried in
it all) thumb

my tattered Emerson looking
for the words/ finding
no need for words . . .

just

lying back with you be-
side me as

the golden song plays
over us . . .
!

## Child-Lady / Child-Man

Old
cello against the wall once
filled with music of
your long black-bearded
lover who

planted a flower in
your womb for
your natural childbirth (more
beautiful than anything from
the belly of his
rich deep music box)

you (skin
wrapped in fantasy animals this
early morning) as
last night you were
wrapped in me

taking
our love cups from
the head of the bed to
fill them with morning
coffee/ you

smiling
beneath your round glasses over
your fire blue skylight eyes
my child-lady (how

appropriate for me/ your
child-man)

> "Something
> very intimate about New York" / you

say (thin

girlishness in
your voice) as
the neighbors vent their
hangover through your
floor (your

old lover as
a hangover in
the cello by the wall/ you
now I hope a bit
drunk on me) church

bells initiating our
new beginning from
the Church of Ascension on
5th Ave./ our
fresh song (cello
quiet in the dust) some-

thing very
strong and natural and
simply beautiful about
this childbirth too

your
array of bright beads hanging
from a mirror on
one side of the cello

your
wild bright skirt (crocheted from
rainbow scraps) hanging
by a hook on
the instrument's other side

perhaps
you'll wear them today as

we spread our
dawning music like

a red sun dancing
children over the East River this
magnificent

today . . .
!

## Loving You on My Birthday

Depression
eating away between
my ribs leaving

nothing but my
emptiness
lying
beside you as

my 39th birthday ends/ sky
weeping all day over
New York City/ Fritz'
memorial service

impotent
unworthy of love/ of
being loved

knowing
you cannot really
love me (corpse of
your dreams) still

you lie hold-
ing me/ your
smile warm-
ing my cold flesh re-

viving me/ New
York City re-
stored/ my

laughter
rising above the
Empire State Bldg/ my

arms of strength and

love reaching
out to embrace all
Manhattan with
my manhood

all
faces pressed so
happily in

your endless
tiny
womb . . .
!

## Sunday Breakfast

How
pleased I am with

your dark smoldering sensitivity in
the mystery chasm of your
big round glasses/ your

strong gentle sculptress' hands with
soul in stone in
the Whitney/ your

deep marmalade piled
so happily on your
crisp black toast/ your

insecure disguise so
transparent like a clear glass robe
hiding
so unsuccessfully your beauty/ your

tender laugh at
my tiny handwriting (so
big with love for you) the

little child in you like
a bag of baby clothes (you
too fearful to unpack and
discard them/ afraid
to lose that identity) you

so
unwilling to acknowledge your
reality in your sculptures/ your
poems/ your
9-yr-old William/ so

unwilling

to find yourself laughing through
my own joy right now

so
unwilling to release all this in
your daily movements (afraid

they are not worthy/ still
relying on the glass robe/ your
lonely fantasy that
it shields you . . . . )

Jeanne love
how
happy I am to be here at
your table staring

at you/ into
you/ being
you

. . .

over

the fruit and
coffee and
Sunday *Times* . . .
!

## Small Crisis

Billfold filled
with telephone numbers of
fading hope/ no
dimes left for calls anyway

my
essence in a pile of
poems/ all
I am or ever
will be in

a small room on
14th St./ no
postage to get them out to
be read/ dim

light fading/ my
poems about
to walk the streets with
the rest of me/ you

Jeanne
about whom they've all been
written telling
me

"Jason is
so erotic, he
never stops . . . . "

my
poverty lying beside you in
my penis as
deflated as my billfold/ as
my poem/ my

manhood gone to putty

"With Jason there's no care but
with him it's
always sure orgasm . . . . "

me
wanting to wrap his
golden fleece around his balls and
jerk his instant orgasm clean
off/ all

my strength wrapped in
frozen steel ripped from
my breast and
gagged in my throat

*Fuck*
*Jason!* but
of course, you do . . . .

"Fritz, you
arouse me more than
any other man . . . . "

and
we hold each other/ dust
slowly melting from my
anemic smile/ still

my billfold in my pants over
your chair across the room
filled
with telephone numbers of
fading hope/ no
dimes left to call

all
I am or

ever will be against
you now returning from
a long cold distance as
you speak

"I'm sorry, I
guess I was
getting even . . . . "

long
cold winter thawing from
my throat making
its way to
fill the hollow chasm in
my breast

(perhaps
tomorrow, yes

my darling, hold
me, please, my

dearest Jeanne, just
hold me
now
. . .
!)

## Happy Loafer

spread
across the bed of
all my love like

warm butter sopped
con-
tentedly into bread/ me

the happy loafer sapped
of everything but
a pleasant sat-

isfaction (loafer heated with
your fire fresh
from your oven) how

nice
it is loving you with
nothing left to

care or
do/ nothing
left but lying on your

plate for
your grand feast/ how
yum

yum (very
yum
      yum

            . . . . )
                      nice . . .
                                !

### 3rd Week

Spar-
row on our
3-wk-old birthday card from
you/ thrush

terribly dignified (no-
where close to 3 wks just
trying to make it through
the winter)

my
winters so mild now with
you boiling the snow and
seducing the wild Norseman with

your steam smile (poor
winter warmed
to milquetoast in
your breath) only

spring left/ whole
world a garden of
wide-eyed buds on
our 3rd birthday/ each

day a few more sprouts/ another
tree swimming blossoms
breeze singing . . .
Jeanne . . .

through the tall grass making
the fields dance . . .
Jeanne Jeanne . . .
bending

the trees with grace/ washing
the oceans up onto

the shores with
gentle fingers . . .

Jeanne
Jeanne
Jeanne
3-wks-old today (have

I known you every
second/ every
moment before that to
lead us to

our thrush
so
soft and endless
everywhere in his

3-wk-old
song . . .
?)

## 2:00 a.m. Awakening!

Roach
circling the table/ carrier
of my rage exploring
the basket of
oranges and bananas

2:00 a.m./ you
Jeanne, having awakened me
fire
engines singing
New York disaster/ my

disaster/ clarion
of anger ripping
weeping down
the cold cheeks of
14th St./ why

did you awaken me
you
repressing your own anger wrapped
in a bright towel/ why

did you awaken me from
my peace freed
of the shrieking of
my own despair/ my

manhood burning from my
waspish guilt/ my
incapacity to break the
seal of depression and
put myself to work/ my

stomped-out desire to

try anymore/ me

the carrier of song/ why
should I care/ why
should
the roach weaving his
meaningless patterns
concern me/ why

Jeanne
do you (like Brutus' Lucius)
work about the kitchen
getting
my coffee when
you should be sleeping/ why

for godsake did
you awaken
me?

"Because I want to
make love . . . . "

fire
engine quiet now/ strange
sickness creeping through me
street
wet with dying snow covering
my groin

"Go to bed, Lucius!"

morning
seeping gray over
the East River

the
Ides of March and



nothing I

can or care to
do . . .
!

## My U.S. Constitutional

Bottom
glued this morning to
the seat re-
leasing its passion in-
to your bowl, Jeanne

all
of yesterday's oral
satisfaction culminating in
this grand rejection
whole

bathroom reaking with
delight/ asshole gone
berserk creating
great long sexual fantasies to
wallow in your

tepid pool/ all
my anal glory like
a regatta of brown
submarines surfacing to say
thank you

thank you, darling, for
our magnificent weekend all
ending in this
beautiful ritual of
the end *from*

the end now
recording every word and
turd upon
the roll of paper on
the wall/ everything

wiped clean, my darling, as

the plop thickens in
our game of life (much
to get upon my fingers for
me to sniff our pleasure all

day through the streets of
New York) O
fecal madness through
the outhouse of happiness and
I rise to

pull the chain and
watch
my poem dance upon the water and
get sucked into
the mainstream of life (O

Jeanne, my
beautiful sweet Jeanne, you
so much the succulence of
my never ending end/ this
ceaseless flow

I
drop my trousers and
grunt
grunt . . .
seat myself again to

grunt
grunt
grunt . . . . our
incessant
joy . . .
!

## To Give You Thought

Monday on
the steps of the
Advent Lutheran Church covered with
rice from a weekend
marriage and

my rear end scarred from
yrs of
sexual murder/ me
wanting to scoop the rice into
my pocket to

take it home to Jeanne for
her to boil (with
my dirty linen) that

I
might partake of a
bowl of decency (my
Chinese yen for
better things) as

people walk smiling past me on
spring-draped Broadway
New York City giving
birth to
a new warm season/ all

her faces dragged up from
the ice to
thaw
with me this bright mid-
afternoon/ sun

licking
its yellow tongue happily through

my army jacket (no

Jeanne, I
can do without another
marriage but

the thought of it puts
your smile on
the sidewalk and
makes the cement a
little softer for the

3 tiny children climb-
ing around me chortling like
helpless mice . . . as

their mother stands
futilely by nursing
a baby cart . . .

! ) perhaps if
I
just wash my bloody hands and
clean my skin-filled nails I

can scoop up some of
that good rice and
throw
it on your doorstep/ some-

thing to give you
thought . . .
!

## After Dinner

House
quiet but for the
piano soft-

ly crazy to my rear ca-
cophonous with
Jeanne's 9-yr-old William sing-
ing as he draws in

the bedroom to
the Alka Seltzer ad on
his TV/ Striker

the old red dog wheezing
through gray whiskers
vague

NY sounds from
12th St. siphoned through
the bldgs at
the rear of your
5th flr walkup

all
together somehow in
some mad symphony (with

interjections of
a fire engine and
crying child . . . . )

like
the wire basket of
fruit before me tinted by
the purple-shaded lamp

bananas

pears
oranges . . . yellows, greens
reds/ in-

effable harmony as
William plucks the strings of
his father's cello (Striker

pushing
open the bedroom door re-
creating the balance) no

reason to this harmony in
the aftermath of
dinner chaos

but
all so real/ whole
city singing endless
voices in and

through me
now . . .
!

**When You Ask if I Shall Ever Write You Another Poem**

You
changing my diapers (now
with 39 yrs of soiling to
account for
their great and purposeful
load) then

pressing your face to
my graying mustache (every
bit as weighty and
well-seasoned as my
diapers) how

can you, Jeanne dear (so
delightful in your
lover's role) be

un-
aware that every
song that I have ever
made (from
soiled to loving) has

sprung from your
flower garden (true
you've only come across this
blooming phenomena in
the past 4 wks but

does
that make it less
true?/ are

you so easy to deny a
fire on the
far side of the sun just

because you haven't walked
it?) well

Jeanne love
you walk it now/ 4
                            whole
                            wks of
your garden burning (as

indeed
it always has and
always will/ all
your red hot roses that
you may choose to call
                               Fritz) all

39 yrs in just 4 wks
the Fritz flower burning at
your feet/ no

end to this song/ just
a ceaseless singing/ never

to go out this
fire flower (what

                  joy for your
                  sweet window

                  box . . .
                  !)

## Me/You Song

Ly-
ing back upon
your bed/ 2:00 a.m.

darkness all
around and through me
in-

separable as
the me and
you/ being
me/you - us

right now/ be-
ing
the night/ all

of everything this
vast blindness
swim-

ming through us as
a current passes through
a minnow guid-

ing the small fish down-
stream be-
ing the end of

being (O
my darling
how

wonderful this/ how
grand and
                beautiful this

holding you/be-

ing nowhere/ every-
where/ all

there is/ all
to be and
will in

us/ in
all of us right
now . . . .

### Restoration!
*for my father*

Roach
crawling slowly up my
wall toward a letter nailed
there like my flesh from

a publisher about my
poems " . . . they
represent a decadence that
I loathe . . . . " then

on
to a hanger hanging from
a spike/ roach
stepping gingerly through
the blood/ hanger
bereft of accomplishment/ cars and

trucks grinding
14th St. below my window/ their
ritual of impotence working
to their graves

my steam
radiator hissing to explode/ song
of execution at dawn as
the roach explores the hanging ground/ a

poem by my son (then
12) living
with his mother in Greensboro away
from me for
yrs

> "I have teased my father
> for a long time now"

and

another by
my ex-student

“ . . . calmly turning
within the emptiness of broken cups” and

I
am legless in my bed/ my
candied gams chewed off by
desuetude freshly

butchered (were
they bought with food stamps . . .

?) and
my heart like a dried
prune rests upon
my manly woman’s groin (which

you, Jeanne, who
are now beside me take
into your hands to
stroke away the
rage . . . ) and

my father like
an Indian warrior
gray sticks astride my
pony of wild mss holds
a pen and paper toward
me (yes
I know the honor of our
tribe . . . ) and

I take them (new
strength creeping through my
fingers) and

the words like

prairie grass grow
thick upon the paper and

the dirty walls of my
small room become
the sky/ each

poem and note a
songbird with
the roach a

tiny sparrow flapping
through it all so
judiciously sucking

the warm sweet
air . . .
!

**DOWNTOWN POETS SERIES**

*The Invention of Spain* by Ivan Argüelles
*Interesting Times* by Enid Dame
*Sores and Roses* by Fritz Hamilton
*Palaver: West Indian Poems* by Althea Romeo-Mark

**previously published by Downtown Poets Coop**

*For Sex & Free Roadmaps* by Jack Alchemy,
calligraphy by Susan Mashman & Joyce Hobbie
*Between Revolutions* by Enid Dame
*Kanji: Poems of Japan* by David Gershator
*Bang Bang Lulu* by Phillis Manuela Gershator
*Redman is Redman's Mommy!* by Fritz Hamilton
*Jo-Ann in the White House* by Irving Stettner